T0132122

Everyone Can Be
POSITIVE

BY
GERTRUDE MEEKS

Illustrated by
Shomaree M. Potter And Cynthia M. Potter

Copyright © 2009 by Gertrude Meeks. 575933

All rights reserved. No part of this book may be reproduced or transmitted in any form or by any means, electronic or mechanical, including photocopying, recording, or by any information storage and retrieval system, without permission in writing from the copyright owner.

This is a work of fiction. Names, characters, places and incidents either are the product of the author's imagination or are used fictitiously, and any resemblance to any actual persons, living or dead, events, or locales is entirely coincidental.

Text copyright © 1995 by Gertrude Meeks
Illustrations copyright © 2005 by Shomaree M. Potter and Cynthia M. Potter

Book Designer: Junnar Sanchez

To order additional copies of this book, contact:
Xlibris
844-714-8691
www.Xlibris.com
Orders@Xlibris.com

ISBN: Softcover   978-1-4257-5026-8
             EBook   978-1-4771-8083-9

Library of Congress Control Number: 2006911236

Print information available on the last page

Rev. date: 04/20/2022

Dedication

This book is dedicated to GOD who inspired and enlightened me with the vision to write this book of feelings. HE also guided me through the journey of actualizing a wonderful gift. Through GOD's guidance, HE placed people in my life that encouraged, believed in me, and trusted me. Cynthia Potter and her son, Shomaree Potter, were GOD sent in my life. Their extraordinary artistic souls captured the wonderful characters of this children's book. They will continue to be a shining light forever in my life. I thank my husband, Kevin, my daughter, Latoya, and my two grandsons, Michael and Mekhai, for their enduring love and patience. I also thank my mother and father, Florine and Woodgee Smith, my sisters, Cleo and Stella, and my brothers, William, Godfrey, and Michael for their continuing support and encouragement. Finally, I want to thank my fore bearers who instilled the values and strength that has come down through the generations and to also dedicate this book in loving memory of Emma Louise Dunston.

With heartfelt gratitude,
Mrs. Gertrude Meeks M.S.Ed.

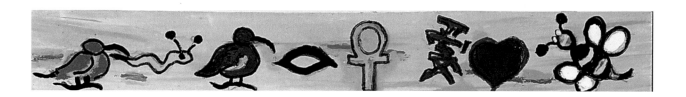

In the land of feelings,
there appeared a little girl
whose name was Positive.

Positive liked to make everyone that she knew feel good.

One day, Positive was talking to Sad. Sad said, "I'm not happy."

Positive said to Sad, "We are all special and can do special things, like doing something nice for someone, saying kind things to others, and treating everyone special."

This made Sad feel good about himself.

Sad told Positive, "I know some people who would like to feel good about themselves."

"Who???" said Positive.

Positive and Sad went to visit Angry.

"Hello Angry," said Sad.

Positive said to Angry, "Hello Angry, would you like to feel better?" "Yes," said Angry.

"Angry do you know that we are all special?" said Positive.

This made Angry feel good about herself. Then, Angry said to Positive, "I know someone who would like to feel good about himself. Let's visit Hurt."

Positive, Sad, and Angry
went to visit Hurt.

Positive said, "Hello Hurt, would you like to feel better?" Hurt said, "Yes! Can you tell me how to feel better?"

Positive said to Hurt,
"We are all special"

Hurt told Positive, "I just remembered someone who makes all of us feel good like you do, Positive.

"Let's visit Love…"

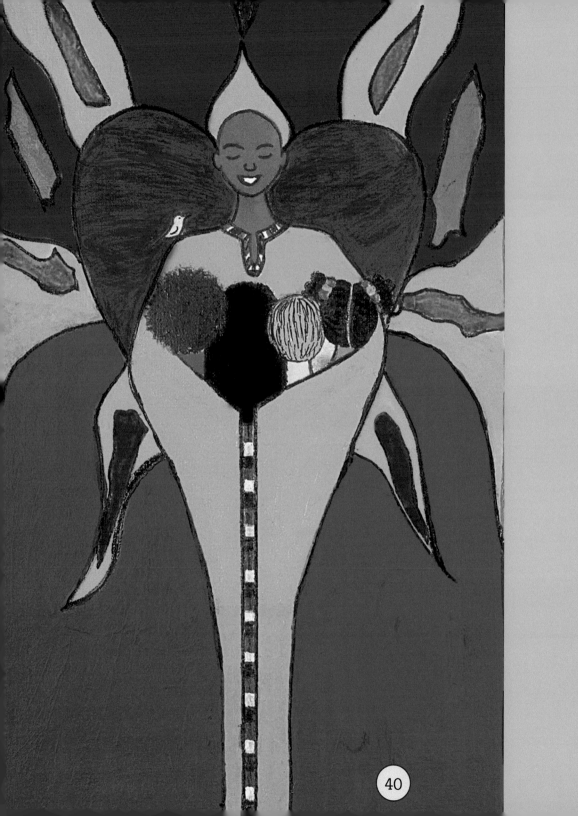

Love said to Sad, Angry, Hurt, and Positive, "You see, everyone can be loved and love others.

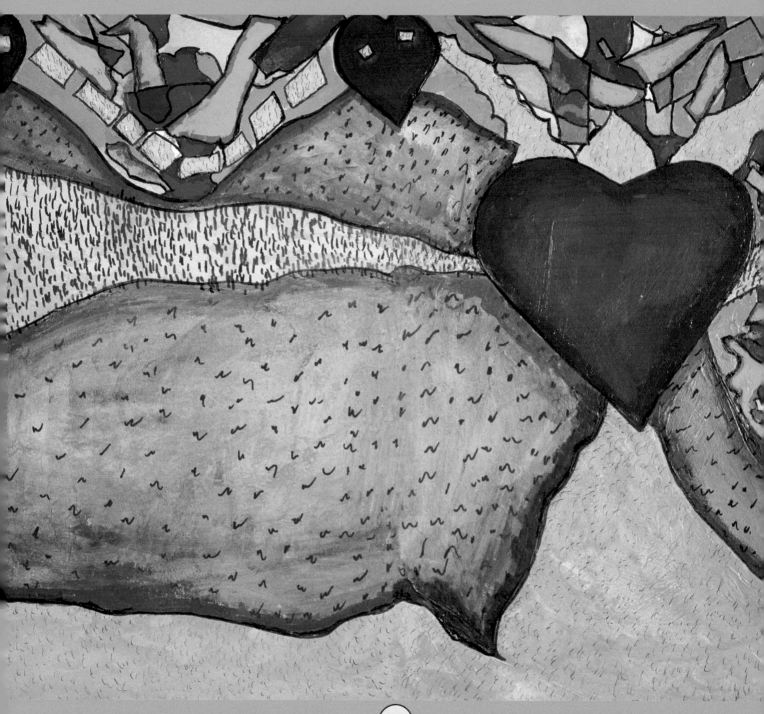

Special Notation

   Thanks to our ancestors and parents, Percel C. Harris and Nancy J. Williams Davis, for their nourishing love and fresh memories which will continue to live.

   Special thanks to Willis M. Potter, husband and father, for his collaborative support.

Affectionately,
Shomaree M. Potter-- Illustrator
Cynthia M. Potter-- Painter

Printed in the United States
by Baker & Taylor Publisher Services